Dogs, pubs and living with MS

Good Days, Bad Days

M.Winship

My life

I was born in July 1950. Now 66, I am a pensioner. My family consisted of two brothers and four girls, one being myself. I can write this book with my partial sight because it is black and white, and has bold print. I feel so good about writing this book myself, as I never thought in my wildest dreams that I could do this.

We had no electricity when I was growing up, just gas mantles on the walls. My sisters and I would often read by a small paraffin lamp, and after falling asleep would wake the next morning and find we had very black noses. Even though we were poor, I enjoyed my life. We had an old coal fire that was very large; three quarters the size of one wall with two sides and the fire in the middle. The toilet was in the back yard, and had a piece of wood across with a hole in it. The coal house was in the back yard too. In the toilet were newspaper squares hanging on a string from the pipes. It was really cold in the winter going to the toilet; there used to be icicles hanging from the toilet roof it was that cold.

What got me growing up was that there were no cuddles, or mentions of 'I love you'. It must not have been done in those days. The comment to children that you should 'be seen but not heard' got to me.

When I went to infants school all of my sisters and brothers wore sandshoes, and when we got a hole in the bottom of them, my father would just put thick cardboard in them. Then, as we got older, we got good sandals from Clarks shoe shop, and a white bonnet at Easter.

I remember when I was three, my sisters took me across the road to a neighbour's house – they had the first black and white TV in the street; it was a Rediffusion. We watched the Queen's coronation and I loved it so much.

At home we had a tin bath in front of the fire. We used the kettle to warm the water for the bath, and two of us used to get in at the same time in front of the coal fire. In the living room Mam used to heat up the water in the large 'poss tub' for the washing, she would use the dolly stick, then she would wring the clothes out by hand. Later on she saved up and got an electric twin tub.

We had no fridge, just the pantry in the scullery and we had a single room for the two boys, a double room for us four girls, and Mam and Dad were in another double room. The boys got the coal in and the girls washed the dishes, dried them, and put them away. My sisters used to take the mickey out of me because I got so cold at nights I wore my nightdress and my dressing gown, so when I woke up my face would be shining with sweat and I had my eyes open and they used to laugh at me and I said I did not want to miss anything, that's why I used to have my eyes open. I remember a note on the stairs one Christmas Eve saying: 'Please watch the stairs down to the toilet as they are very slippery, take care, Love Santa Claus xx'.

My family – my eldest sister, my nephews, and my great-nephews and nieces – live on the Isle of Wight. I do have a great-nephew and great-great-nephew in Peterborough. I don't see any of them very often as I cannot get decent disabled facilities where they live in Newport. I have looked into buying or renting a property in the Newport area, but everything is so expensive for a person like me, and I have a beautiful house where I live. I have the beach at the bottom of the road, and the shopping mall in the town centre is nearby at the end of my street. I keep thinking about how I love my home as it's all adapted for me, but I do miss my family a lot.

I used to shop for the old people in my street when I was a kid, and in return they would give me a little money to spend on myself which I was so grateful for. The fairground and the music on the town moor (Hoppings) was always good, I used to love it. But the poor goldfish we won were always dead by the time you got off the moor, they had white spots on them anyway. I think they probably bred them in bulk, and that their quick death was planned so that you went on the games again.

It was so funny, once I was having a conversation with a young friend and I was telling her about the outside toilet, and the newspaper for the toilet roll that used to hang on a piece of string from the pipes, which was cut into squares, and that I had a piece of string to pull in order to flush. My father always took the tissue paper from the baked bread that mother got from the bakery as he refused to use newspaper. You should have seen her face. "Did you not have toilet rolls?" she commented. "Not when I was a little girl," I said. We didn't know any different in those days. We were able to leave our front doors open and all the neighbours were friends. Nobody bothers anymore.

My favourite game growing up was pouring candle wax down the back lane and sliding on it. My next favourite game was 'Jacks', I was good at that. We made snow igloos, played 'paper chases' around the back lanes and 'knocky nine doors', and we would put the bin out and play cricket with a ball and a piece of wood.

When it came to bonfire night we used to dress a 'Guy' and go up to the main road and get a penny for him. We used to get 'London lights' and sparklers, and we were able to watch everybody else's fireworks. We loved to pop the blisters from the bonfires on people's back doors the next morning. We also loved baked potatoes from the bonfires.

The surfers were always in the sea at Tynemouth Long Sands.

I was watching 'Loose Women' recently and one of them admitted she got chewing gum off the road. I was amazed because I thought I was disgusting because I did it too!

Sunday dinner at Cullercoats Beach was egg and tomato sandwiches, and roast beef sandwiches. That was when beef was cheap. We used to make a table out of the sand and put a tablecloth on the 'sand table'. We then went across to the wooden hut to get hot water so we could make a cup of tea. We used to have to take the small sieve for the tea leaves as you didn't have tea bags when we were younger – whether you could get them or not we wouldn't have been able to afford them. We would then go to the rocks and pick winkles so we could cook and eat them when we got home, and my Dad used to get crabs' legs to eat on the train when we went home.

The beach at Cullercoats was used by smugglers in the old days as it had plenty of caves there, but they would have had to time the tides carefully as at certain points of the day they can be full of sea water.

Going along to the fairground there used to be all of the fishermen's wives selling their products outside of their cottages, and Mam would get some mackerel for tea. We would walk to the 'Spanish City' along the seafront and go on some rides, then we would put tuppences in the machines – it was like 'Tipping Point' on the television, it was so good! Sometimes we would go to Tynemouth Long Sands to the outdoor swimming pool. They had girls' beauty competitions on there;

they were great but the water in the pool was freezing cold. They are getting a smaller, heated pool built, but I bet it will not be as much fun.

I do not know how my mum used to feed us in those days, but she was a good cook. Sometimes she would whitewash someone's ceiling to go and buy a small loaf of bread for us and put jam on it. There was a pie shop around the corner called 'Williams', I think they used to sell them at Newcastle United football matches. They were lovely and sometimes we would have pie and chips for tea.

The ragman came down the back lane on his horse and cart one day and the horse had a poo on the road. An old man ran out of his back yard and shovelled it up. There was a young man leaning on a wall in the back lane who saw the old man and shouted at him, "What are you going to do with that horse poo, Mister?" The old man replied to the young man that he was going to put it on his rhubarb! The young man was disgusted and he shouted back, "Yuk! We put custard on ours!"

I used to get some tomato boxes, cut them up for bundles of sticks for people's fires and sell them for money. Sometimes I would take newspapers to the fish and chip shop and get free chips. (There was once a man who walked into a fish and chip shop and asked for 'Rocky II', and the shopkeeper told him the video shop was around the corner, so the man went around the corner. The man went in again the next day and asked for 'Death Wish I', and again the shopkeeper told the man "the video shop is around the corner". The man left. Then the next day he walked in, and before he said anything the shopkeeper said to the man, "We are a fish and chip shop, and that's what we sell." So the man said, "OK, I will have a bag of chips." After a minute he said, "You wouldn't happen to have a Fish called Wanda to go with those chips, would you?!") Then I would go around people's houses and get their empty pop bottles so I could take them back to the shops and get money for them – it would pay for me to get into the pictures that day!

Young people nowadays would not know how to do things like that; they would be too busy on their mobile phones. It annoys me, hearing the bleeps all of the time from the kids texting; there is no conversation anymore. We didn't even have phones in our houses in the days when I was growing up; you had to use a phone box in the streets. And we didn't have calculators, or a computer – we had to use our brains.

We were always around the radio, I used to like 'The Archers' and 'Desert Island Discs'. On a Sunday night it was the 'Top Ten' on

'Radio Caroline'. We did not have electricity, instead we had gas mantles. When it came to Christmas we put candles in little trays, and we would hang them on the trees at the ends of the branches – although we never lit them. We would also put coloured paper together to make decorations for the rooms. The best presents I got were the 'Bunty' and the 'Broons' books, and the camera that showed 'Yogi' and 'Boo Boo' bears on a white sheet on the wall.

We used to holiday in caravans at Blyth and Crimdon Dene in Hartlepool; it was great. There were gas mantles for lighting in the caravans as well. I used to have relations in Dunbar, Scotland. I loved that place. They had an outdoor swimming pool with beauty pageants on too.

The first job I had was when I was around fifteen-and-a-half at the 'Co-op' store on Buddle Road in Newcastle upon Tyne. I had to pass an exam to get that job, but it was a good wage. It was an old fashioned shop, and I used to go down to HMS Calliope on the Tyne with 'Co-op' groceries on a bicycle. It was hard work getting down to Scotswood Road and back up to Buddle Road stores – I must have been fit in those days, it was like Granville in 'Open All Hours'.

I would also parcel up in brown bags items such as mushy peas, rice, sugar, lentils, split-peas, and so on, and I used to weigh and wrap butter and cheese in greaseproof paper. Eventually I was promoted to 'Cakes and Bread Manageress', and would order the bread and cakes. I loved that job. At the end of the day if the food had not been sold we were given the chance of taking it home – which we did!

When I was growing up it was the time of the 'Beatles' and the 'Monkees'; I loved the music from both bands. As I got older it was Motown that I loved.

I got a job in the Blackett Arms Pub in

Newcastle when I was eighteen. It was one and two pence a pint of scotch, and two and nine pence for a bottle of Brown Ale. Alcohol was cheap then. I used to get back home about 3 o'clock in the morning as I didn't finish work until 11 o'clock. From there I used to go to a disco called 'La Dolce Vita', where there were good groups on in the night-club downstairs. Then I would return home on the late-night bus, and my father would shout at me from his bed, "Late again!" One night he got to me, calling me a prostitute, even though I was still a virgin at eighteen. I didn't tell him when I had sex for the first time. I was drunk as hell and had gone back to this guy's place for coffee. All I remember was falling asleep on his bed, but when I woke up at 4 o'clock in the morning I found my clothes on the floor. I got dressed and walked about six miles home in the dark by myself. I couldn't stop worrying that I might be pregnant because your family made you give the baby up for adoption in the 1960s – but thank God I was okay. My father was obsessed that we would not turn out like his mother, who prostituted herself with the sailors on the boats in the Tyne. Eventually, she left her husband and her four sons to go and live in a hotel in Liverpool. I always thought my dad was the only son of my grandad; I didn't know my father had brothers, so I might have had cousins somewhere. I never knew my dad's dad, as he had died before I was born, but I was told that he was a lovely man. My sister received my dad's mother's death certificate, and it said she was a spinster. She must have been some kind of woman to do what she did.

Then I moved to London, stupid me. I was told it was paved with gold. It just shows how naive I was. The first night there I slept on the benches in Trafalgar Square, it was 1969, and I got a job the next day with accommodation.

I was a barmaid in The Strand in a pub opposite the law courts; it was called 'The George' and was positioned just down the road from Fleet Street. I used to watch the trials – they were so interesting. I would try and have conversations with people in the pub, but they did not want to know me – or maybe they didn't understand my accent, I don't know.

Then I moved to Streatham; the people there were very friendly – so different from the centre of London – and me and my younger sister worked at the Oval cricket ground as barmaids at the weekends. It was good there, but I also worked in a fruit shop during weekdays in Streatham high street. We had a room in a large house in Streatham, but it was so expensive to live in London.

I once met a guy who was deaf and dumb. I couldn't understand how he was such a good dancer until I found out he could feel the vibrations – he could always read my lips! He invited me to his house for tea and I met his mam and dad and twin brother; they all had the same disability as my boyfriend. When I got to the front door I didn't know how I'd get in, but I managed to anyway. He knew I was there as the lights flashed on and off; he was so intelligent, a solicitor.

I went home to Newcastle but I had to hitch a lift as I did not have the money to get home any other way. The guy who gave me the lift was weird so I kept my distance. He picked some other girls up too and he gave us all a ride home to Newcastle. Once back, I got a job as head barmaid at the Royal Oak Hotel at Keswick, Derwent Water.

When I was 22, I went home on holiday. There I met my husband, he was a friend of my brother's and we got engaged, and later, married. A year after the wedding we went to Germany to live in a private flat – it was a dirty place in Horde Dortmund as we had to wait for army accommodation. When we got our army accommodation it was a lovely two bedroom flat in a tall building. It was nice in Germany, and it was so funny having two New Years as there is an hour's time difference; the food was good too!

There was a favourite Sergeant Major I met so that when I had been shopping at the Naafi he would march the prisoners out of the guardroom, and then march them back in with the shopping and look after it for me until I came back to the guardroom. He would then get a taxi to take me home, and the prisoners would put my shopping in the boot of the taxi for me. I went to a German supermarket one day and asked for eggs, but the shop-assistant told me she didn't understand. So I squawked and flapped my arms like a hen, then I put my hands behind me to pretend to catch an egg. She brought me some toilet rolls instead. I said no, laughed, and walked out. I went into another shop and I wanted a pastry brush to put egg on my pastry. Again the shop-assistant said she did not know what I wanted, so this time I drew a picture. She came back with a paint brush and a broom. I said no, and thought just give up. I used my fingers to put the egg on my pastry instead. I also went to the German cafe on the camp and asked for a ham sandwich, but it was wafer thin bacon, so I left it.

Then we came back to England and I worked in a few pubs in Hythe, Hampshire where I got some good references.

I trained to be a publican at the Rose and Crown on Newgate Street in Newcastle, and passed. The first pub I was given to manage was the Imperial Hotel in the Bigg Market, Newcastle for Wadds glaziers. It has taken me forty years to go back and visit. I had the pub for two and a half years. I used to stand at the gate and stop the large line of people coming in. The street is completely changed now, from my old pub, The Imperial Hotel, down to Balmbras Music Hall, along with a lot of other public houses that have been turned into cafes or coffee shops. I used to go to Balmbras a lot, as Viv (Geordie Gill) used to be the manager of the Imperial Hotel two reliefs before me. That man was so nice, he used to go in Balmbras as well. It was from Balmbras that those heading out for the Blaydon races left, and so it was named in the song ("I took the bus from Balmbras"), then out along Collingwood Street, and onto Scotswood Road. I hadn't been back to Newcastle because of what happened to Viv; he had gone to his favourite place, a pub called The Azure Blue (owned by Geordie Gill), and he was stabbed and died.

The Imperial Hotel has gone now along with all of the pubs to the bottom of the street, even Balmbras. It has all been ripped down now for a nightclub. There is another nightclub on the other side of the Bigg Market, so some of their business might go. The street was all foreign cafes, most of which were shut, and it was dirtier than the time I worked there. I was so upset. There is a round toilet underground that people want to make a cafe out of; knowing what it was I would not want to eat there. I shouldn't have gone, I was amazed it had changed so much. When I had the Imperial Hotel I would stand at the gate, which I kept closed, and the young lads would beg to come in. I said no, as I was only allowed so many in for fire safety reasons. So I told them "two out, two in", and they went away. The place was always packed, I cooked dinners there and I got loads of customers from the Evening Chronicle Newspaper. They were the best customers, and their favourite meal was my homemade chicken pie. I had a job keeping up with it all. The staff used to give the printed orders to my dog who would come downstairs and stand at the kitchen door, then he would give the order to me and go straight back upstairs for more orders. The men came in soon and asked for protection money and I said no, that I would rather give the pub up, and I mentioned a few names of hard people I knew so they disappeared. The staff I had were really great and they were so hard working, we all were happy. We had fancy dress nights and other funny things, it was great.

The places down the Bigg Market, Cloth Market and Groat Market are a dump now, it is such a shame. The biggest mistake I made was to give up the Imperial Hotel, as the next place I took on was 'The Coach and Horses' in Blenheim Street, Newcastle. I was promised so much and I was told I could have the catering and the flat upstairs. I bought crisps one day and she went mad. I never got either of the things she promised me, especially the flat upstairs. The customers at 3 o'clock shut the doors for a lock in, she must have allowed that, the people staying. So I stayed open for a while longer – which in the end lasted for 16 hours – then I closed up, gave her the keys, and left. I should never have left the good pub I had, and what I experienced was not what she had promised me.

I was then offered 'The Chieftain' at Cruddas Park, Westmorland Road, Newcastle. It was named after a tank that was made by Leyland motors in the 1960s. I got beaten up twice in that pub – I was pulled over the bar by my hair (which was torn out) and then punched and kneed in the face. The woman who attacked me pleaded not guilty at the Magistrates Court, and it took six months to get to Crown Court. By this time she had gotten herself pregnant, and she received a £1.60 fine for the breaking of the glasses, and a two months ban from the pub. Even though the police were present it had seemed a waste of time, and she was in the pub toilets again that night.

The toilets themselves were so bad; graffiti all over. So I bought a proper cleaner, and washed it all off. I went back in later and it was all back. I had a nervous breakdown in that pub. I didn't tell anyone because I didn't want the people to think I was frightened of them. One night, I was open at 6 o'clock and a man came in with a black top hat and black coat on. I asked what he would like to drink and he said he was only there to pick up the manageress' body. I said he would have a bit of a job as I was still alive – it was then I realised he was a funeral director. I explained to him that there was a guy that I had just barred, he must have called because he did not want to drink, just use the phone, and I had refused. He had lost his temper so I had pulled the plug out. The staff came in later and I told them the story. The fire brigade came next – we heard the siren ringing – in they came looking for a fire. Then we would have an ambulance, and then the police, and so it was. It was like F.Troop coming in. The fire brigade asked me if I would go and listen in to the call that had been made, so I agreed. I told them it was the same person I had just barred, but that I didn't know him or his address.

I had my large glass windows smashed everyday by kids throwing bricks at them. I said to the breweries that it would be better getting plastic windows in, as it would work out cheaper. They agreed, so I had them put in the next day and it was great. Shortly afterwards a guy came in and I told him he was not getting served, so he picked up a heavy stool and threw it at the window. He didn't know they had been changed, and he was not a happy man as the plastic windows made the stool bounce back and hit him on the side of his head. Me and all the staff had stood behind the bar and laughed so much that he threw glasses at us; he then went to the customers' tables and turned them over too, then he left.

The next pub I got was 'The Ford Arms' in Byker; it was full of some awful people. They used to spit at me and throw winkle shells at me. They stabbed the manager seven times in the pub across the road; he lost so much blood. They were shouting, "Your turn next!" So I closed up that afternoon and didn't open that night. I phoned my area manager and told him to get me another pub, or I was going to another brewery, and they were good enough to take notice.

He got me a pub and hotel by the beach in Whitley Bay. I worked 16 or 17 hours per day, seven days a week. I loved the place and the customers so much that I worked there for three years. I used to put buffets on for darts, the police, and weddings. The hotel was good, it was full of Navy lads, HMS Coventry, and they were great people. I held jazz nights, which were so popular, they were amazing. The people enjoyed it so much – one of the ladies from Tuxedo Junction sang on the jazz nights, she was very good. One of the jazz nights I had, there was a baby grand piano, drums, violin, double bass, a saxophone, and a trumpet playing. It was a busy night! On a Friday and Saturday I had a compere who got the audience up to sing; his name was Patrick Healy and he was good. The poor man is dead now – he died around 1982, the Falklands War was in full swing, it was so sad.

I had a long music lounge and we had a baby grand piano. There was live music seven nights a week, and during Sunday dinnertime I had two women. One played the piano, and one played the violin. They were called

Minzi and Mena. We were packed for Sunday dinners. I used to give them what I would like myself, and how my mam used to do things. The singer of the group 'Lindisfarne' came in every Sunday for his apple crumble and custard, he loved it. I used to have Halloween parties and put up spiders and skeletons and make people get dressed up for first and second prizes. I would make a big pan of broth with ham spare ribs, and sell two ribs and broth and a piece of stottie for £2 per ticket.

We had good Burns nights too, and I would sell haggis, neeps and tatties for £2 per ticket, and first and second prizes were whisky. We also had a piper to pipe in the haggis and recite the poem. One Burns night the weather was so bad in Scotland with snow they could not deliver the haggis, so the Scottish and Newcastle Breweries had it flown down. I was so pleased because the tickets had been sold and the piper booked, so I was able to have my Burns night!

Christmas was beautiful, with decorations and a free buffet in all the rooms. I had my two German shepherd dogs who both knew the time to come out of my flat, and who would bark and go behind the bar for their crisps. There was one long haired and one short haired dog – Shep and Heidi were their names. One day the long haired dog chased a customer into the toilets and my husband came up the back lane and saw the guy shouting out of the toilet window for help. Shep would have licked him to death if he had come out, probably thinking it was a game. My husband got hold of the dog and let the customer out. The dogs would come out at 11 o'clock every night and go behind the bar. One of the dogs – the short haired one – took prawn cocktail crisps, and the other dog liked salted crisps. It amazed me how they would always pick the ones they liked, and the way they would go and lie on the floor outside the bar and eat them all, bursting open the packets with their paws, The customers used to ask me how I paid for things, so I would tell them how I bought the meat tickets every week, and that the money I got from that paid for everything. They could not believe it.

I had a bar with a dartboard, and a darts team that I once went to a club in Benwell with. But they did not let women buy their drinks on their own, so I told them my team would not be back and I walked out. I had a pool table in the bar, and a buffet and music room upstairs. Above that I had two floors in the hotel and a kitchen upstairs. My friend from Malta came to visit me one winter. I went there on holiday every year and my sister looked after the hotel for me while I was away. So, I treated her to a holiday in Malta one year. It was a lovely island with lovely people, and the food was very good. My friend came one Christmas; he had a cafe on the beach at Mellieha Bay which was always packed. Tables and chairs on the beach were hard to get. My partner used to ask, "Have you got a plate of jockeys' whips?" instead of chips; his son asking what they were when he used this saying in front of the customers. We used to laugh when we heard him say this. His dad used to take us places in his speedboat and posh car. They were such a lovely family and we were invited to their house quite often. It was a beautiful house in Schembri, and was cool because of the marble design. The second day he was in Whitley Bay it snowed so he had to go and buy some boots. He said it was the first time ever he had seen snow and was chuffed to bits. He brought with him another hotel manager from a large hotel in Malta, named 'The Topaz' in Bugibba, and they stayed four days in my hotel. I was so pleased, and surprised, when I saw them standing at the bar waving at me, since they had not told me they were coming. It was nice to be able to do things for him for a change and it was good to let him stay at the hotel. He lived in Qawra and I used to go on holiday to the old Bugibba Town in Malta. I loved it there: the Maltese were such nice people. They went through a lot in the Second World War and so did not like the Germans.

After three years in the pub and hotel, I took a guesthouse over with my brother. He was a silent partner so I did all of the cooking and serving. I think it was then my MS (Multiple Sclerosis) started. My brother wanted to sell, and I found buyers for the guesthouse, so he got his money back and more than he would have got elsewhere. I was holding onto everything as I walked, and then I started dropping everything. I could not seem to feel things, even the very light things, and it really got me down. I would get so frustrated at the amount of things I would drop and I would think to myself, "not again". The tremors in my head and my hands are really bad now, and with the Trigeminal Neuralgia my sight is bad. I am in a wheelchair now and have to depend on people. The multiple sclerosis has really progressed. So, my then-husband and I got a mortgage out and we bought a house in Whitley Bay. My husband and I wanted a Karaoke machine, and as he sang I put the tapes in the machine. I got the gigs for us, and when he was tired I sang instead. We were popular and got quite a few jobs, so it kept us in money until I got a part time job as a receptionist at a television repair shop. One day the phone rang and they said they were at Cowpen, and as I was telling my boss he said it was pronounced 'Coopen' in Blyth.

I found out I had MS on October 31st 1999. Although it was the optician who found out I had something wrong with me, because my eyes shook as well, he said he could not tell me anything. I used to have to hold onto things to walk and would get so tired, so I went to find out. I was told about the MS and then, after being in hospital for a day, was told I had Nystagmus and would be registered blind. I asked the optician if I was going to be totally blind, so that I would not see colours anymore, and he said no. He said I had cataracts on both eyes, so I asked for them to be removed. He said ok, but that it would be about three months' wait, and because of the tremors in my head he would have to do it under general anaesthetic and I would be in hospital for a few days. The next thing they did was to put me in hospital for a steroid drip, constantly sending students in to do tests. It was the Royal Victoria Infirmary in Newcastle, and I told them I did not want the students to come in anymore as I was so tired. One of the things I do not like about MS is having a bad memory. I know exactly what is in my mind but sometimes the wrong words come out, and I feel so stupid. One of my regular carers knows what I want to say; her name is Cath and I love her as she cares so much for me.

I also have two best friends who help me so much nothing is a bother. Their names are Kay and Ray. When my dog was alive they looked after him for me, but his kidneys failed so they took me to the vets to put him to sleep. I cried so much. I absolutely love dogs – they call me the crazy dog lady. Another thing I hate about MS is not being able to walk; I am always looking out of the window at people walking, remembering when I could walk. I had urinary sepsis twice and was taken to hospital both times by an ambulance, where they put me on drips and a strong antibiotic drip. I was there for four days. I told them at the hospital that I wanted to be home for the holidays at Christmas, so they let me go home. The second time I had sepsis I had a high temperature and high blood pressure, but they let me leave the hospital after two days. As you can tell, I do not like hospitals, as with my sight problems I can hear every noise in the ward and it makes me jump with fright.

Although I am partially sighted, and writing this story has really hurt my eyes, I am a person who is very independent, so I keep on going. I hate the dropping of things, and the tremors in my head and in my hands are really bad now. I find I cannot swallow or talk properly as I choke on my saliva, which my doctors say can go down into my lungs. When you have MS I find that a sense of humour keeps you going. I have Primary Progressive Multiple Sclerosis – that's the last stage you can have. The worst test I had was a lumbar puncture. They took fluids from my spine while I was awake, and when the tremors started they gave me a tablet to calm me down. This worked, but late that night the headaches were terrible, so they gave me tablets and said the headaches would have been caused by the procedure. When my speech was slurred people used to think I was drunk; but since I do not drink or smoke this made me angry. It is funny how I could sing OK, but after a while I could not sing at all. I got really annoyed with myself as I loved singing. There were two young men there when I was singing at a Karaoke night, and as I staggered along with my walking stick they laughed at me. I went to the toilet, then came back and told them I was not drunk, but had a disease. I said that I hoped they would get it too, and walked away. I could not get over it since I do not drink now, much preferring water. I was so angry at the lads, but I should not have said what I did. MS is bad in the north-east, but is worse in Scotland because of the colder climate. When I got MS my husband left me first, followed by all of my so-called friends – so much for

29 years of marriage. I was told, by people who have MS, that this is what happens. I was told to keep my sense of humour, as it keeps depression at bay. I was in two minds as to whether I should try being a comedian or not, because when I was in the pubs I was so good at telling jokes. But, I have a bit of a bad memory with the MS, so I would have to write them down as a prompt. One day I went out with my enabler and I asked for hair dye with no pneumonia in it, instead of ammonia, and another day when I said to my carer, who was at my house, that I should have urinated the meat overnight, when I meant marinated.

The good thing about my tremors was the shaking since it used to keep a head on my beer – only kidding!

You have to laugh about things and keep in mind that there are people worse off than you. I take about 31 tablets a day – prescription and herbal. My carers keep me in touch with the world; I love to talk to them, because I feel so lonely otherwise. I love dogs, but since I cannot have one now I have treats and squeaks for all of the dogs that I see down the promenade at the beach. There was one day when I gave a very small dog a squeaky and all I could hear was squeaking along the promenade. It was having a great time. I cannot afford to get a dog walker as they charge £10 per 50 minutes, which is a lot of money. I regret not doing the things I could have done when I could walk and could see better. I have a needle phobia, so if they want blood I tell them not to say "sharp prick" but just to put the needle in, because it does not hurt as much this way. I went to Canning Street infant and junior school until I passed my 11 plus and then I went to Pendower High School. I left just before I was fifteen, just wanting to leave for a job and get some money. I was a bowling addict: I loved to bowl. Now I roll my ball down a metal ramp, but at least it reaches the skittles. I used to love Whitley Bay, but most of the Scottish people do not come anymore and most of the pubs have closed in South Parade. The Spanish City has closed now and most of the shops have closed on the seafront; the town has changed so much. Every Sunday I used to go to the quayside under the Tyne Bridge. The shopping there was great, and I used to love the lifts on the Tyne Bridge, though they are not working now. There is a beautiful new bridge across the Tyne called the 'Millennium Bridge', and one day I hope to see it. The town centre in Newcastle is great; I used to love the Grainger Market, it was so old-fashioned and had great food in it.

As I get older I realise I have not done all the things I wanted to do. So everyone please do them now, because you do not know what tomorrow brings, and if you have not done them you will regret it.

When I was younger I used to walk everywhere. I would walk all the way along the River Tyne to the park at Ryton Willows, and to the swimming pool in the park, where I would go swimming.

I used to walk to school all the time – even in the snow – and to all of the jobs I had. Nothing bothered me.

I am proud that I am a strong and stubborn person, so that even though I have Multiple Sclerosis I still potter through.

Even though this has happened I have a lot of good memories from my life, and no regrets.

Even though I liked to have many drinks in the pubs, when I got ill with my MS I stopped this. It did not bother me to stop drinking. Now and again, I have a can of McEwans Export on special occasions as I love it, and used to drink bottles of this when I was younger.

I like small amounts of food, though I only go out twice a week. It is amazing, because what I could not afford when I was younger I can get now. I am not big on the lower part of my body, but large on the top part; with having to transfer from my wheelchair I now use muscles I never knew I had.

My old pub, 'The Station Hotel', has been pulled down now and made into flats. Before it happened I would have loved to have seen it one more time.

I have a lot of good memories of that place. Although I've never seen ghosts I was told they were there, so when I went to bed I used to say goodnight to everybody. There were people who asked me if it was haunted. I would tell them that I had never seen anybody, but others had. Someone had once seen a little girl in a pink crinoline dress sitting on the stairs of the hotel; she was there one minute and gone the next.

Imperial Hotel,
Bigg Market,
Newcastle, 1977

Costume party at the
Imperial Hotel,
Bigg Market, Newcastle

Jazz night at the Station Hotel,
Esplanade, Whitley Bay

*Me, seven years old at the back
with my sisters, Blyth*

*Christmas party at the Bigg Market
at the Imperial Hotel, Newcastle*

Me, 17 years old and cousin Elaine Gibson,
18 years old, La Dolce Vita Night Club

Wonder Woman fancy dress night, Newcastle

Me at the Chieftain, Cruddas Park, Westmorland Road, Newcastle, 1980

Me at award day, Scottish & Newcastle Brewery

Station Hotel, Whitley Bay, 1982-85,
built as a hotel in 1836

Me, 23 years old, Hythe, Hertfordshire

My wedding day

Shandy and Albert on Mam's back stairs

My wedding day

Me and my barmaids dressed as saloon girls, fancy dress night at the Chieftain

Me and Shep at the Chieftain

Melrose guesthouse, Esplanade, Whitley Bay, 1986

Me (seven) and Gina (five) at my sister Norma's wedding

Robbie at seven weeks old

Robbie in the back yard, three months old

Robbie and me on the step at home

Robbie before he died, 1981. Wet after swimming

Robbie

Robbie

Me with Heidi and Shep

Shep

Heidi and Shep   *Heidi*

"Now try and get past me," says Shep

*Me and my friend's
dog, Dougie*

Shep

Robbie

Crazy Dog Lady

The first pet that I had was a hamster at the age of eight and I bought everything for it that the pet shop told me I needed. I had saved my pocket money up and did lots of odd jobs for the neighbours to get the money. I called him Zeus. I loved watching him go around on his wheel, and I got such a shock because I did not know that they stored food in their pouches at the sides of their face. At first I thought he was going to get fat, the speed at which he ate! He got a large lump on his side, but we were so poor that my mum could not afford to give me an advance on my pocket money. So, I took him myself to the vets' around the corner. The vet said my hamster had to be put to sleep, and I said I would do any jobs he needed, to pay for what he charged, but he put him to sleep for nothing. I cried all the way home; I loved that hamster so much.

It was the time of Yogi Bear and Boo Boo, and I got two mice – male and female. I called them Pixie and Dixie, and they mated. So, I had twelve little babies and, when they were old enough, my school friends bought them from me. After I was told that male mice sometimes ate their babies, I had to buy another cage to put Dixie in. I still do not know if it's true or not, but at least they all got good homes. They were lovely colours: grey and white like their parents, and some all white.

After they had gone I got a tortoise. I kept him in an egg box with newspaper at the bottom and let him walk in the backyard. I used to put new newspaper in his box on the scullery bench. I was told tortoises were colour blind, but I did not believe that since he headed straight for the tomato sauce. I kept him indoors in the winter so he could hibernate in the straw I had put in the box, but after a while there was a smell, and Mam said he had died.

One night I was walking on the pavement next to Condercum Field. It was starting to get dark and I found a very large toad going up the pavement next to the road; it was the size of my hand. I was frightened that it would go onto the road and get run over, so I caught it and took it home. My mother went mad and said get rid of it, so I took it back to the field and let it go, hoping that it would find its way home.

The next pet I got was a cockatiel. I let him out quite often, but it was so hard to get him back in the cage, and he bit me quite a lot, so I gave my cage and food to a neighbour as she wanted the cockatiel.

When I was young I used to fish for

tadpoles, not knowing at that time that they turned into frogs. Then my friend and I went frog collecting, letting them go back to where they came from when we had first caught them. I would catch red bellied stickleback fish at Leazes Park in Newcastle upon Tyne. I would take them home in a jam jar, but I should have put them back in the lake, as my mother would put them down the toilet and pull the string when I got home. She was a tough woman. I was not very knowledgeable in those days, as you can tell. When I got older, I thought nothing of looking for caterpillars or black beetles under rocks, spiders or snails too, but now I am scared of these things. The next thing I bought was the runt of the litter – a black, male mongrel puppy. My sister decided to get the sister, which looked a bit like a German Shepherd. I told my sister that my mother would not accept two dogs, so we hid them under the bed in our room. My black dog was so intelligent and he learnt all of the commands very quickly. I used to walk all over with him. I got married to a soldier who was posted to Germany, so my sister, who lived in the country, offered to look after my dog for me.

I got one of the army guys' budgerigar, but as he did not want it I took it back to England. It was so tame that they called it Twinkle. I used to love it. An officer was taking his parrot back, so he offered to bring her back to my house for me. Twinkle was allowed to fly anywhere she wanted, but when we came back from shopping one day she was missing. We looked everywhere for her. We shouted all over the house but could not find her. My husband went to a breeder of budgies and got me one, and when we put it in the cage, we heard a tapping noise. It was Twinkle; she had fallen in a thin flower vase.

I got her out and she was okay. She spotted

the new bird in her cage, looking in her mirror, so got back in her cage and pecked him until he moved. I took the other bird back but refused to take the money back; I said the owner should give it to the kids, and that they could spend it on whatever they wanted.

The gentleman took the bird back OK and I felt better that he had gone back with his friends.

When I got back to England I got Shandy, my dog, back. We moved to Hythe, down South. I was an army wife, and we used to walk along Southampton water at high tide. I would walk barefoot through the water, and when we got to the vets in the town Shandy would cross the road. He hated the vets, so you cannot say he was not clever. There was a kitten that lived next door to us and a large dog would often try to attack her. When this happened, Shandy used to chase it away. The kitten was always in my house with Shandy;

she loved him.

I used to get Shandy to get his dad's slippers, and he would go and get them one at a time and put them in front of his feet – so clever. Anything I wanted he carried for me; one time he even brought my budgie upstairs to me. I screamed at him to drop Twinkle and he did so immediately. The budgie was not hurt at all. When Shandy was down on the floor the bird would go over and peck at his feet. When my husband left the army, and we went home to Newcastle, he jumped the fence in the back garden. It was New Year's Eve and the snow was horrendous. I went to look for him and I squeaked his toy lots of times but I could not find him. I went to the rescue centres the next day, put adverts in shop windows offering a reward, rang all of the taxi companies to ask them to keep an eye out for him and put adverts in the newspapers, but nothing happened. I never knew where he went. I was broken-hearted: for at least a year, he had slept on the right hand side of the bed, so I still put my hand down as if to stroke him, for at least a couple of years after he went missing, but he was not there.

The next dog I got was a long haired German Shepherd that had been at the rescue centre for a long time, since nobody would take him. The owner of the centre said he had a lovely nature and that he would let him out. I was halfway across the yard when he came fleeing towards me and put his paws on my shoulders and licked my face, So that was it – he melted my heart. I told the owner I would have him. While the boss of the rescue centre filled out the forms, I was talking to his very old cat which came and sat on my knee. The owner said that in the time he had had the cat, no one had managed to get it to go on their knee for a cuddle. He said he was supposed to check my house out first, but because his cat had come to me he gave me a leader and let me take Shep home. He had one ear up and one down. I was told to wrap his ear, and that it would come up in time, but it did not. It gave him character, though. I had a hotel and he would stand at the door of the hotel with me and he would give the kids a paw. He did this for the blind society charity. He raised £199 at the time. I took home the sandwiches that were left and put them on the bench – only to forget about them. This was until I found them down the pillows on the settee-chairs. I also found butter and bread, so I thought he was going to make his own sandwiches! It was not as though he did not get fed. He got his food, and treats too, such as Dentasticks which cleaned his teeth. I did not know about separation anxiety, so something which happened that was my fault was when he broke the glass on the front window with his head, crossed four main roads and walked down to my work to look for me. I was busy at work, and joked to my husband, "What a day to bring the dog down!" But he said he had not brought him. I thought we had been broken into, so we rushed home in the car. The greengrocer over the road from my house told us what had happened: he said he could not believe it; the dog had leapt out of the window and there was no way he was going to stop him. I still do not know how he got to the pub as he had never walked down with me before.

One day he disappeared, and it turned out he had gone down to the butchers and got his usual large marrowbone. I could not think where he got the blood on his paws from, he must have buried it on the way home. And he had crossed a main road again. My back garden was like a graveyard with his marrowbones, I am sure he was a mole in his past life as, he was always digging bones up.

When I went down for my meat the next week, the butcher told me he had been for his bone the week before. That's where the blood had come from, and he had buried the bone on his way home. In the end his back legs went and I had to have him put to sleep. The last thing I had seen was Shep looking at me sitting in the car as my husband carried him into the vets; it was as though he was thinking to himself 'why are you not coming, Mum. I will never forget that stare. I felt so guilty not going with him; I can still remember that stare.

The other dog I got was a short haired German Shepherd that his owners did not want. I said I would take it as I used to have Shep then, and if he would take to her I was happy and he did, so I got a very skinny dog called Heidi. She was a nice dog who needed fattening up. I gave her everything to try to eat, but she could not put on weight, and then a farmer said to try wheatgerm tablets and they started working after just a week. I had Heidi spayed and Shep castrated; she was the alpha, and did she not know it. Shep and Heidi loved to swim in the sea – he went first and Heidi went second, hanging onto Shep's tail. She was dying at four in the morning, so I called my vet to come and put her to sleep, but she died on my lap before he came at eight o'clock. He took her body and said he would get her cremated and give us the ashes back but the crematorium said they could not find the ashes so I was really angry and asked for my money back – but the vet still charged me £50 to come out plus cremation charges.

One day Shep chased a man into the toilet of the hotel I was managing. He would only have licked him to death, but my husband was coming up the back lane and the man was shouting 'help' out of the toilet window. It was funny because Shep would not have touched him; he probably thought it was a game. However, my husband ran into the hotel and got hold of Shep and then got the man to come out of the toilet. He said he had been in there for an hour.

The next pet I had was a large terrapin. He used to take his food under water so I had a strong filter but it still smelt, so I took him back to the pet shop and swapped him for goldfish. At least they lasted a long time and they were relaxing.

He was eight weeks old when I got him; he helped me to get through Multiple Sclerosis and my husband leaving me for another woman: my next dog was a beautiful Border Collie who I called Robbie. He had a white heart on his head, white on his legs and black elsewhere. My ex threatened to take him but I said no, so I told him I would take him to court and I got to keep him. He helped me get through the bad times. He was so clever. They say dogs do not see colours, but he knew every colour frisbee he had which were green, yellow, pink and blue. He would stand at the gate waiting for the kids to come, and the children in the street used to play with him all of the time. They would get any colour frisbee they asked for, and he would get it and throw it over the gate for them and they threw it back for him. The kids loved him and he loved the kids. He loved swimming in the sea or lakes but the mother swans did not like him beside their ducklings; they would hiss at him although he was not interested. When I got MS my friends Kay and Ray looked after him for me. They even took him on holidays with them and took videos and photos of him for me. When he was 12 years old he got kidney failure, he could not drink, eat or walk. My friends took me to the vets to put him to sleep; I was broken hearted. I was never able to look after a pet again. So they were my beautiful pets – I hope you enjoyed it, as much as I have had remembering the good times I had with my beautiful pets, especially my dogs.

Where I live

We have a large 'Angel of the North' as you come into Newcastle. This statue is so popular it gets a lot of visitors; you can see it from the motorway.

There is a lighthouse on the beach where I live. It was once called Bait Island after the gentleman who once bought it was called Mr Bates and he sold bait to the fishermen. Once upon a time there was a Chapel there dedicated to St. Helen and all of the monks were killed there. There is a burial ground next to the chapel that used to be there; the monks used to put a light on in a window so sailors could see there was an island there to keep the mariners safe. There were often smugglers in the Bay; it makes me wonder if it was them who killed the monks or whether it was a disease.

On the cliff edge at St Edwards Bay the Vikings came; they came over the sea, and climbed up the cliffs from the beach. The Vikings came and murdered the monks of the Priory and raped and pillaged the village of Tynemouth and took all the items that were worth anything from the Priory at Tynemouth and the village.

The next beach along, Cullercoats Beach, had smugglers' caves as well but they would have to have been aware of the tide times as the caves on the beach used to fill with water.

The town is very interesting; it has a quayside along the Tyne river – that's the song Jimmy Nail sang about, the Big River. He was in the TV programme about workmen in Germany who were from the north east of England, Auf Wiedersehen, Pet. I live about 12 miles from

Newcastle.

There is a ferry that takes people across the Tyne to South Shields on the Gateshead side of the water. The Chinese restaurants are in Stowell Street in Newcastle, and they have a Chinese New Year with guys dressed up in a dragon outfits. At the bottom of Stowell Street, are the city wall remains, belonging to the outside of the castle, where the villagers would have lived.

The town of Newcastle is interesting too, it has a magnificent cathedral well worth seeing. St Nicholas. There are a few old Victorian streets going down to the river Tyne that are so interesting too.

It also has a castle built in 1080 by William the 1st, which the Normans would share with William's son. I think William wanted castles in the North. The bridges we have got are the new Millennium, Swing Bridge, the High Level for the railway and pedestrians, and the Tyne Bridge, that Sydney Harbour Bridge took a copy from.

The Great North Run starts off over the Tyne Bridge and ends in South Shields. This half marathon is run every year and people come from all over the world, with a lot of local people running for charities. Everyone gets a medal at the end of the run.

The street I live in is called Alnwick Avenue, the next street is called Warkworth Avenue and the street after that is called Percy Avenue, which was named after the Duke of Northumberland, the Percy family who owned the land. Alnwick and Warkworth are two castles in Northumberland and Harry Potter was filmed at Alnwick Castle. About an hour's drive from where I live. I think the houses were built for use by the workers who worked on the lands at the time.

We have lovely beaches including Tynemouth Long Sands, where people do plenty of surfing. Whitley Bay beach is the beach where Vera, played by Brenda Blethyn, was filmed once on the promenade, seafront and the Links. She was originally from Ireland but she is good at our Geordie accent.

We also have Blyth beach where they hosted the tall ships in 2016. They sail into the Tyne through the piers at North Shields and they were at Newcastle a previous visit and they stopped at the quayside. Then there is Seaton Sluice which has a beach with a lot of sand dunes.

Up the road we have Bamburgh Castle and the beach is lovely. There are flats in the castle now. Holy Island can be seen on a bright day from there, but it is well worth a look; it's fantastic. Seemingly El Cid was filmed on the beach there a long time ago, with Charlton Heston as the star playing El Cid. We have Holy Island, with Lindisfarne Castle and the Farne Islands with the seals and birds, which is very interesting. You have to take a boat out to the Farne Islands from Seahouses. The Vikings came to Holy Island across the sea in their long boats, and killed all of the monks in the church there and stole all of the things that were of any value. You have to watch the tides over the path to Holy Island, as there are only certain times you can cross as the tide comes in so fast over the causeway; it has shelters that you go in to escape drowning. There is a beach called Druridge Bay in Northumberland, and the sands are wonderful.

I live beside Segedunum, part of the Roman Wall at Wallsend and if you go on a long way up the West Road where I used to live there was an altar in the garden of a house, and they would slit animals' throats and the Romans would offer these to their Gods, and if you carried on up the West Road, there are a lot of ruins of the Roman Wall. The American Kevin Costner played Robin Hood, Prince of

Thieves, with Morgan Freeman in the film of
that name. It was filmed at Sycamore Gap on
the Roman Wall; it was a great film, well worth
a watch. Then onto Housesteads a Roman fort
and museum which is great to look at. There
is also a place called Vindolanda, both near
Hexham, then look out for Hadrian's Wall
itself – the wall was 74 plus miles long, built to
keep out the Scottish barbarians. There was a
film made about the ninth legion. There was a
fort on the wall where the Roman soldiers left
from, to get their Eagle pennant back. They
went over the Scottish border; most of the
soldiers were killed, but there were a few who
lived in the woods, and they went to help the
Roman soldiers from the fort, but everybody
did get killed and they lay beside their Eagle
Pennant – whether it is a true story I do not
know.

Then on the west coast was where Beatrix
Potter wrote her children's books, about some

wonderful animals. She died and left all her property to the National Trust. Also in the Lake District William Wordsworth wrote the Daffodils poem, and more; he wrote most of his poems at the back of his home as he got a lot of inspiration from the beauty of the Lake District – and who could not get inspiration from there as it is so stunning.

Around the corner in Monkseaton, near where I live, there is a pub called The Monkseaton Arms. It was called that because it was a brewery once upon a time and the monks from the Priory used to make their beer and mead there. They would walk from the Priory at Tynemouth in an underground tunnel which had a stream in it, so they used the water from the stream to make their beer.

Lightning Source UK Ltd.
Milton Keynes UK
UKHW020911050619

343908UK00009B/281/P